CALLED OUT

T0158164

CALLED OUT

Open letters to those most important to me . . .
as my beeper beckons me for the final call.

RONALD D. ROBERTS, MD

iUniverse, Inc.
Bloomington

Called Out
Open letters to those most important to me …
as my beeper beckons me for the final call.

iUniverse books may be ordered through booksellers or by contacting:

iUniverse
1663 Liberty Drive
Bloomington, IN 47403
www.iuniverse.com
1-800-Authors (1-800-288-4677)

ISBN: 978-1-4759-3769-5 (sc)
ISBN: 978-1-4759-3770-1 (ebk)

Printed in the United States of America

iUniverse rev. date: 07/31/2012

INTRODUCTION

I recently heard a successful author comment that he had trained extensively at the finest schools in the art and technique of writing. His life to that point, however, had left him devoid of ideas about which to write. I suppose that I find myself on the opposite side of the street. I feel saturated with ideas and life experiences but lack any formal training in writing.

I will have no time to seek training in writing. Life is quickly slipping from my earthly body. I'm not strong enough to even sit at my computer; I'm using a pencil, eraser, and tablet. There may not be time for revision or proofreading, yet my mind is clear and fertile with stories which need telling, perhaps only for my sake. On the other hand, perhaps there are a few out there who would find comfort in the knowledge that a living God will take an active role in one's life, that the American Dream is within the grasp of all of us—even a mailman's son! Someone might even find amusement at exploring the patchwork of human frailties and emotions which constitute a medical doctor—perhaps much like their own.

My format is one of a series of open letters to those who have meant the most to me during my forty-six-year journey along the road of life. Few of these dear people need a letter to know how I feel about them—and that's as it should be. Perhaps I should admit the obvious—these are really letters to me, about them. It is for my benefit that these memory boxes are reopened. I am comforting myself with old gifts from fellow travelers.

Should a talented editor or writer undertake the task of resurrecting these ramblings into literature worthy of publication, I would be honored. If any family member, loved one, or friend finds some pleasure in reading these letters, my reward would be more than sufficient. Or should it come to pass that I am the only one cognizant of these penciled ramblings, I've still had fun!

AN OPEN LETTER TO
THE GUYS AT THE GYM

Had they been doing fetal ultrasound in 1945, there is a good chance that the study on Hazel Roberts would have projected a nine-inch sphere patterned with grooves, an air valve, and VOIT stamped across the broadest surface. The remaining fetus would consist of chest, arms, and legs (and hopefully ample penis) clamoring to assume the defensive position. The subsequent delivery of this orange *basket-human* into the state of Indiana sealed its fate. From infancy to my terminal condition at this time, the mere thought or mention of basketball sets forth a surge of passion and emotion far beyond reason. Throw in an *Indiana* with the equation and I'm no less than a fool.

Like so many jealous lovers, basketball has shown to me her best and worst sides. Moderate speed, quickness, good court awareness, and a reliable shot carried me favorably through many skirmishes. A five-foot-nine-inch frame endowed with only modest strength and clearly riddled with "white man's disease" left me dead in the water at other times. It has truly been an up and down relationship, but the love affair never faltered.

As a young boy, I would spend hours throwing rolled-up socks at paper bags nailed and taped to my room walls and doors, imagining my participation in sweltering rivalries from around the area. I accepted my missed shots as well as those made, alternating between goat and hero at the supper table, much to the bewilderment of my parents. Neighborhood critics were constantly amused at my makeshift square, wooden backboard-rim combinations (rarely approaching

1

ten feet in height) which were the target of countless tosses of my old bladder-style basketball. Round steel basketball rims and mats were simply not in the budget. I'm sure the scenario was even more amusing to neighbors (and probably my family) upon finding my hoop creations flat on the ground after any significant windstorm.

Virtually all free time involved milling around pick-up basketball games hoping the older guys could work me in for a game. When success occasionally reared its head, I would spend hours reliving my performance in vivid detail. Elementary school leagues and teams became colossal events in my life.

Things got deadly serious in junior high school. Teams were chosen by tryouts—many tried out, and fortunately, many were kept on the team. There were only a few games and I saw little action from my lowly spot on the roster. This is a point in my life where I began to exercise a faith and philosophy that have served me well to the present time. I prayed to God for some type of break or chance and I committed every available free hour to repetitions of shooting, dribbling, and footwork.

My chance came as we were getting drubbed by a sixth-grade all-star team during our last game of the season. I was inserted in the third quarter and proceeded to score and pass as if I were a starter. The game remains a blur to me, but it set the tone for me to succeed as captain of our eighth-grade team and a frequent starter on the freshman team (a team composed of all three junior high teams from the year before).

Tryouts for the junior varsity signaled the potential end for would-be varsity players at Bloomington High School. Getting cut at the JV level would not bode well for a future varsity career. Approximately two hundred candidates of vastly mixed ability showed up for a shot at the twelve varsity and twelve JV positions. We had a week of drills and scrimmages to prove ourselves. The pressure was unbearable. I felt that I was playing well, but that nobody was noticing. Specifically, I felt that the coaching staff was preoccupied with the "name" players who were already destined to make the teams and play major roles.

The last evening of tryouts, I was calling Dad from the outer gym office for a ride home. Dad made the mistake of asking how I did ("You made it, didn't you?"). I was distraught to say the least, and I launched into a tirade about not getting a fair chance; that I was always forced to scrimmage with the "scrubs" against the good players, etc., etc. Suddenly, out of the adjacent coaches' locker room burst Mr. Huff, the JV coach. Eyes glaring, Mr. Huff wasted no words in setting me straight about having been fairly evaluated and about my mouth and attitude. I ate no supper that night, sitting on a stump in the backyard hardly noticing the October chill. I cried and prayed. Most of all I knew that I, by myself, had blown it.

The cut lists were posted after school the following day. My miracle was emblazoned across the final JV roster—*Ronnie Roberts*.

The JV year was certainly no picnic. I was, at best, one of the last two players on the roster. Playing time was rare. My spirits remained high, however, as I saw myself getting good coaching and thoroughly enjoying the camaraderie of the road trips. Mr. Huff was actually a neighbor and frequently drove me home from practice. I never came up with the nerve to ask him why he didn't cut me that night after my tirade.

We had one game left in the season (at Evansville Bosse) and I was playing too poorly to have a shot at making the travelling team. I went to see some friends with my parents that weekend and ended up playing a bunch of pick-up games with junior high kids. I stunk so bad that I wasn't about to announce that I played for a JV team. Returning to practice Monday, I had the feeling that I was entering my last week of organized basketball—I suppose I was pretty loose. At any rate, I could not miss a shot all week. I was unconscious from every point on the floor. I not only made the trip, but shelled Bosse for a few rainmakers.

My last week of JV ball set the tone for the following year. Those of us with aspirations for making the varsity literally lived together on various basketball courts around Bloomington and at the IU HYPR building. We became *one*, both on and off the court. Tryouts for varsity were almost predetermined, although Coach Rhoades did tell me that I was "the last guy I thought would ever come up and make my team."

The year was frustrating. Mostly seniors played, and they lost big. We juniors (six in number) knew that we were the hope for the future and we were expecting a "youth movement." It never came. We ended up losing to a small school (having an excellent year) in the sectional. More frustrating was the paucity of experience for next year's team.

We spent the summer as we had the past. In addition, we were growing. Our front line went 6'8", 6'6", 6'4", and two others at 6'3". I was still 5'9" but was depended upon to move and distribute the ball and hit the open shot.

That senior season typified basketball in my life. Home games were a walk for us—we lost only one. Road games were brutal. For whatever reason, Coach Rhoades saw fit to start me frequently and play me a lot on road games, but rarely use me at home. I felt that Suzanne, my friends, and the home crowd figured that I was a rarely-used scrub, yet I was playing and scoring fairly well on the road. Thank God for radio broadcasts and a few booster bus trips.

My salvation through all this was my close friendship with our 6'8" center, Big Dick. We were inseparable at home, school, and away trips. Big Dick went to Catholic elementary schools and had not been exposed to basketball until ninth grade. He was not addicted to the game like I was—at times I felt that he might prefer not to play. Our talks were about life (girls, school, and motorbike excursions) more than basketball. Big Dick was gentle, sensitive, and fun. It was late in the season and we were travelling to Terre Haute. My playing time was becoming a casualty of a youth movement and I expected little from the trip. What I didn't expect, however, was a sudden wave of nausea and vomiting that resulted in my puking in Big Dick's shoes (always off on the bus) and hat. Rather than become flustered, my giant friend cradled me in his massive arms and the driver pulled into a facility for the clean-up. Big Dick never left me for the entire trip, except while he was in the game. Ironically, Coach Rhoades saw fit to play me during much of that game!

The tournament is what Indiana high school basketball is all about. The last practice before our sectional started, Coach Rhoades called us together, presumably for a pep talk. Then he dropped a bomb. He was bringing up three inexperienced JVs to dress for the tournament in place of seniors, to set the stage for next year. Problem was, we were favored to win this year, and next year was to be strictly for rebuilding. I would have been safe except for my close friendship with a senior who had clearly deteriorated through the year and probably didn't deserve to dress with the team. At any rate, we were both excised from the travel team although we both received varsity letters for the year and appeared on the sectional program. My teammates hovered around my locker for hours after practice, but I was inconsolable.

That snowy Saturday afternoon in the Martinsville gym remains the subject of recurrent nightmares for me. We were well-favored over our bitter archrival (Martinsville was 0-4 on the year) but their sea of obnoxious red and blue rooters made life miserable for us as shots refused to fall, passes went awry, and every call from the referees seemed to injure us systematically. Only Big Dick seemed to hold up to the onslaught (our youth movement was non-existent), but in the end, Martinsville prevailed by four points. My dad literally supported and guided me (my eyes were all tears) down the bleachers, through the red howling mob, and to the welcome silence of our waiting car. I couldn't face the locker room.

I probably came close to giving up on life that Saturday afternoon in March of 1963, but slowly and surely, both life and basketball found their way back. The following season, the six of us graduates picked up a couple of subs and went on to win a state AAU tournament for ages eighteen and under. Our coach was a former IU quarterback, Woody Moore, who convinced me that I was indeed instrumental to the success of this team. I owe Woody Moore a lot. Possibly more gratifying was kicking the shit out of Coach Rhoades' youth movement varsity in the annual Christmas alumni game. I enjoyed one of my best games ever that night ("Where were you last year?"). Of course, I played for my fraternity house, medical school team, and in various leagues through the years. However, nothing has erased the nightmare of Martinsville.

Upon moving to Columbus I began to hack around at a Wednesday night informal league for doctors and pharmacists. Someone noticed me and invited me to join a travelling PR (recruiting) team for the US Marines. This was short-lived, but succeeded in getting me invited to play three days a week with a local collection of former high school and college stars. My acceptance by this group of legitimate players had done more to rekindle my love for basketball than anything I can recall. At about 11 a.m. every Monday, Wednesday, and Friday, I could catch my heart rate quickening as I hurried through the last of my medical rounds, dreading that I might be called into an emergency. Once I entered the fragrant sanctity of the gym, my anxieties seemed to resolve, and I was ready for competition.

The amazing thing to me is that this collection of players collectively amass an impressive array of numbers in distinguished high school and college careers, yet to a man, each has proven to be a real friend—always checking me if I missed a session or two. The games were intense, the fellowship unique.

Well, one day I suddenly found myself at the Cleveland Clinic—seriously ill. One of the first acknowledgements to arrive at my room was a framed poster containing an inspirational basketball saying and the signatures of each and every one of the guys at the gym. These guys are about more than basketball—they are about life, caring, and friendship. Thanks guys!

AN OPEN LETTER TO
MY CLASSMATES

C ompetition for places in US medical schools reached a feverish peak in the late 1960s and remained vicious throughout the Vietnam conflict. I believe that the national ratio in those days reached a high of seventeen applicants per position available (as contrasted with the current ratio of three applicants per position). Many factors contributed to this dilemma for aspiring young medical students. The medical profession was held in high public esteem (this was before the advent of the consumer movement and wholesale malpractice litigation), the Marcus Welby influence promised a fulfilling and hassle-free career, and certainly not least, medical school was one of the very few refuges from the military draft (with likely involvement in the Vietnam conflict and associated atrocities).

The Ron Roberts medical school application (complete with fees varying from $10-$45) found wide circulation as early as 1967. These documents were redistributed annually through 1970. Some institutions were replaced by others from year to year as I carefully studied the statistics and criteria published in the national compendious of medical schools. Some deletions were made because of a lack of application fee capital, while others were made in response to particularly insulting letters of rejection.

By and large, these applications seemed to serve the unintentional purpose of interjecting some levity into the otherwise dreary and tedious sessions of admissions committees. Occasionally, I was even thanked for this. The common denominator with each letter of response, however, was that there was no place available for me in the next beginning class of that institution. My home-state institution, Indiana University Medical School, while obligated to afford me an interview each year, seemed most disinterested of all—to the point that I felt that I was harassing them.

Although discouraged, I was not mystified or angry at what was happening. I knew that these committees were under intense pressure to select the students with the highest GPAs and MCAT (Medical College Admissions Test) scores to fill their classes. Following these semesters of C-work at Indiana University, during which I spent most of my non-class time working and frolicking around my hometown of Bloomington, I finally caught the vision and made the necessary changes to crank out A-work though the remainder of my undergraduate career. The end result, however, was a GPA of 2.85—a far cry from those filling the places in these classes which I coveted. In addition, my MCAT scores were solid but not spectacular enough to overcome my lackluster GPA. All I could really do was serve my time in the military, keep applying to selected medical schools as funds allowed, and pray for a miracle.

My miracle started shaping up in 1969. I was stationed at Fort Dix, New Jersey, in the medical laboratory. Two pathologists, both drafted and hating the army as much as I did, befriended me in a big way. They were sure that I had what it takes to be a good doctor and they began spraying medical schools with very strong and personal letters of recommendation—essentially guaranteeing that I would finish in the top ten percent of any class. These letters found their way to the desk of Harold Haley, MD, a retired army surgeon who was in charge of filling the rather small class at a new medical school, The Medical College of Ohio at Toledo. Dr. Haley had a spot in his head for those serving their country and he was particularly moved by the strong letters of recommendation written by my guardian angel pathologists.

Dr. Haley could not accept me to the next class on the basis of what he had on me, but he invited me to meet with him in Toledo. During our meeting, Dr. Haley suggested that I establish residence in Toledo following discharge from active duty and that I pursue a master's degree at the University of Toledo. He promised to keep a close eye on my performance and to push for my acceptance into the 1971 class if I deserved it.

Needless to say, I followed through to the letter. I was adopted by a wonderful and caring faculty in the department of biology at UT and I completed my requirements for a master's degree with a 4.0 GPA. My problems weren't over, however. Dr. Haley informed me that the composition of the admissions committee had changed. They were "going more by the book" (filling the class with the highest GPAs) rather than looking for applicants with decent grades and unique experiences or personalities. The 1971 class was already filled (without me) but they were expecting some cancellations from students accepted to more than one institution and choosing the other.

My only recourse was to plod along at UT, keep the faith, and wait. I couldn't help from falling into spells of idle reflection—usually recalling the legions of well-meaning friends, professors, counselors, and physician acquaintances who had advised me repeatedly to choose another profession. I would shuffle through my sizable stack of rejection letters like I used to manipulate my baseball cards. My prayers for a miracle were replete with promises to God as to how hard I would work to be a good physician and how I would share the financial rewards.

The miracle took final form in the summer of 1971. The start of classes was fast approaching and my hopes were fading. Then, at some oddball time, a Saturday afternoon, I believe, Dr. Haley called me. His animated voice gave away the purpose of the call as he described an admissions committee meeting which had just concluded. They had two spots to fill and ten files were before them to choose from. My file was included, as usual, because Dr. Haley was trying to give me a chance. Several files had straight A averages from the likes of Harvard and Stanford. My GPA was by far the lowest of the group.

After committee members reviewed the files and prepared to vote, a member abruptly announced that he had recently served as a judge for the oral presentation of term papers by graduate students at UT's department of biology. Dr. Haley quoted him as saying, "We're making a mistake if we don't take Ron Roberts!" The committee followed through, and my miracle was complete.

The remainder of the summer seemed like a lifetime as I waited for something to go wrong. Maybe the school would close, I fretted, or perhaps a state legislator would angrily point out that his son was denied admission with a higher GPA than mine.

When classes did mercifully convene in August, you, my classmates, were bumping shoulders with a four-year-old on Christmas morning dressed in a man's body. The next three years would fly by for me as the forty-eight of us melded into a family. My treasure chest of memories abounds—a few of these deserve rehashing.

My conservative background left me, at best, skeptical about the merits of admitting women into medical school. This bias was reinforced by my ordeal in gaining admission to medical school while watching countless female colleagues eased into medical school classes with apparently lesser credentials than even my own. Whatever problems I was anticipating in relating to my female classmates went up in a poof of smoke at our opening day softball game against the sophomore class.

I remember arriving late and hurrying to change shoes and don my baseball glove and cap. Several classmates had been warming up with a game of catch just adjacent to my car. As I closed my trunk and turned to join in the game, the ball was in the hands of Janet Brockwell. I held up my glove in anticipation of her toss to me. What I got was a vicious curveball which broke about three feet and tore the glove off my hand. My heart has belonged to Janet since that day and I took a whole new look at the issue of women in medicine.

Anatomy lectures began early on and we were divided into teams of four (actually, we "chose sides") and issued cadavers within days of starting classes. Our professor was clearly from the old school (and the old country). His lectures were long and detailed and he referred to the anatomy lab as a "temple of learning." Unfortunately, the team of Roberts, Connors, Walz, and Shook was riddled with irreverence and mischievousness. To make matters worse, our cadaver was grossly overweight, causing the preservative not to penetrate (and fix) the massive areas of body fat, resulting in a putrid stench surrounding our table. The four of us were hardly gracious about our predicament, let alone reverent. We promptly named our cadaver Cleo, because her hair was cut in a manner reminiscent of Cleopatra, and were dubbed "Cleo's Cleavers."

Our eventual solution to the problems of stench and hundreds of tiny nerves, arteries, and veins requiring isolation from mounds of putrid fat was beer. The four of us converged upon the anatomy lab in the late evenings heavily armed with cold beer. Somewhere between a twelve pack and a case, two of us would grab scalpels and forceps and begin to cleave and search while the other two would read directions from the dissection manual (often replete with false directions and confabulated anatomical parts). Hunger would invariably overtake us and someone would go out for fish sandwiches, which were miraculously consumed amongst the stench debris. No amount of scrubbing would remove the foul odors ("morticus disgusticus") from our beings. Practicality dictated that we simply eat while we worked.

Exhaustion would eventually overtake us and we would adjourn to a less malodorous classroom to play euchre and allow our livers to eliminate the alcohol from our systems. Long showers were in order upon arrival at our places of residence. The following day, with relatively clear heads, we attended anatomy lab for the purpose of discovering (and learning) what we had exposed the night before. Our methods were admittedly subject to criticism, but Cleo's Cleavers know some anatomy.

The basketball and touch-football games between lectures, the parties after final exams, Monday night football parties, and do-or-die poker games all served to strengthen the bond between us. So did "class action" acts of irreverence. We didn't enhance our image with administration when ninety percent of the class skipped a visiting professor's afternoon lecture on sexuality to attend a matinee of *Deep Throat* at a downtown theater. I'm sure we looked distinguished to our fellow audience (mostly derelicts and perverts) as we flooded into the front and center seats and proceeded to giggle uncontrollably while alternating between covering our faces and elbowing each other! Not long thereafter, a visiting gastroenterologist, very serious in nature, gave us a lecture on sigmoidoscopy followed by a movie detailing a rigid sigmoidoscopy (using the very uncomfortable "silver bullet") performed on a sweet, fragile-appearing elderly lady. At the termination of the procedure, while still perched in the infamous knee-chest position, the lady turned her head and sweetly articulated, "Thank you, doctor." The classroom exploded in laughter which persisted uncontrollably long enough for our lecturer to snatch up his notes and movie and stalk from the building—never to be seen again. Although collectively ashamed of our behavior, for the duration of our association (including reunions), all of us have responded to every incident of getting screwed over with a simple, "Thank you, doctor!"

Our irreverence continued to serve us poorly during our clinical rotations. One afternoon, about six of us, with our very professional professor, were huddled around a lady with a serious medical problem. We were in a four-bed with the curtains drawn around us and the patient. The room was stone silent except for the soft-spoken comments of our professor. Suddenly, the lady in the adjacent bed let forth with a thunderous fart, which seemed to last for thirty seconds. I quickly riveted my eyes to the floor, but muffled fragments of suppressed laughter permeated the silence. I yielded to the temptation to glance up from the floor only to lock eyes with Brockwell. Her chubby face was beet-red and swollen as she was attempting to seal her oral cavity with a trembling fist. It was all over. Janet and I broke out in raucous laughter while scrambling to find the opening in the curtain for our escape. We were followed by three classmates who had been overwhelmed by the rapid succession of stimuli to crack up. All that remained behind the curtain were the patient, our professor, and a very studious female classmate. We went away that day convinced that our classmate possessed supernatural powers.

Spring fever even strikes in Toledo. I was daydreaming through an April lecture, reminiscing about the fun we'd had during my days at Indiana University when we made our annual trek to the Indy 500. On a whim, I concocted a silly invitation for any classmate so inclined to meet me at the lineup field outside the speedway the night before the race and spend the night after the race at my parents' home in Bloomington. I expected very few takers, but spring fever is a powerful force. There were many.

I suspect that few of us recall a lot of detail from the event. I can call up a vague picture of these white, atrophied bodies frolicking through the night and in the sunshine of race day with motorcycle gangs, undergraduate students, construction workers, and hippies. Many of these bodies were immobilized by excess of beer or wine prior to the parade lap and had to be "collected" for the trip to Bloomington. My saintly parents managed to feed the horde presented to them, but had to call several friends for bedroom space. The group managed to straggle into class Tuesday morning, a little worse for wear, but harboring fond (although vague) memories of their Memorial Day weekend.

Graduation day came all too soon. Somewhat frazzled from the trauma of national board exams, night call, and finding an internship, we all came together for the last time to celebrate our new titles. The day and evening passed in a blur. I can only remember that my long-awaited pride of achievement was overwhelmed by the emotion of loss. I knew that I would sorely miss all of you—and the glorious times we shared.

I still do.

An Open Letter to My Training Mates

"**M**edical school doesn't get it done for you," Paul explained. "You'd better know your shit, but you're light years from being a doctor." My first resident went on to explain that the making of a doctor occurs during post-graduate training. You can choose a program that demands less of you in the way of call, patient load, and patient responsibility—keeping your life fairly comfortable for three to five years. This choice is, however, fraught with a high risk of feeling (sometimes with good cause) overmatched by the rigorous demands of your future medical practice. "Insecurity will haunt you like the plague."

The correct course of action, according to Paul, was to make every effort to get into a traditional, respected, post-graduate program associated with a strong medical school. "You'll get call every third day and there will be many times that you don't think you can cut it, but when you're done, you'll be a real doctor."

Paul Troup's prophesy proved remarkably accurate during my five years of training and twelve years of medical practice. I felt fortunate to be accepted into the internal medicine program at Cincinnati. I also spent the first three years wondering if I could survive it. My patient load was staggering and many were quite ill. Paul was not only super intelligent (I have yet to meet a physician with a greater fund of knowledge), but he worked around the clock, whether we were on call or not. He expected the same from me.

I kissed off my personal life and threw myself into the all-consuming task of making myself into a doctor. I sorely missed my medical school family and the good times we'd shared, but I realized that we were spread all over the country now, never to come together again. Virtually all of my fellow interns and residents at Cincinnati came from big-name schools and seemed far better prepared than myself. I was intimidated to the *max*.

My education included learning a new vocabulary. Demented, ignorant, or cantankerous patients were "Gomers" and their antics earned them "Gomer points." For instance, being found in bed with another patient might be worth four points, while regulating another patient's IV could earn six points. Leaving a trail of stool to the bathroom was big earner, as was starting a bed fire with a cigarette (not uncommon). Patients never died, they "cooled" or "boxed out"; patients weren't discharged, they were "on the bus." In describing a patient's condition, they were "zero delta" (unchanged) or had "the dwindles" (deteriorating).

Morning report was ultra-intimidating. The ward team on call the previous day and night appeared before Dr. Vilter (the program director), the attending physician for the team, visiting applicants for house staff positions, and other assorted dignitaries to present our admissions from our period of call. We had invariably been up all night and few of us had found time to shave or shower. Significant detail was required and pointed questions were asked. You never considered celebrating the survival of an on-call period until the merciful completion of morning report. Euphoria was the prevailing emotion as we filed out of the morning report room to attend to our patients for the day.

On-call nights were endless. While most patients slept, we would work on charts or make conversation with nurses. Eventually, we grew weary of these activities and the team would congregate in a secluded room to fortify ourselves against the oppressive tension inherent with the reality that, at any time, the dreaded beeper could interrupt the silence, announcing that a patient had gone bad or a "horror show" admission was waiting in the emergency room. Many nights allowed me time for congregating while other nights found the bullshit flowing freely.

Each intern entering the program at Cincinnati inherits a dreaded "medical clinic." This half-day-a-week exercise constitutes a significant part of your outpatient training experience. You follow the same patients during your stay at Cincinnati, adding more to the load as you go along. It was common practice to admit patients from your clinic in need of hospitalization to your own team if you were serving a rotation on the wards.

Odessa Folkner (we'll call her) was a delightful, elderly black lady followed in my medical clinic since my early days at Cincinnati. I loved her dearly. When asked how she was doing, she would invariably reply, "Just fine, doctor, just fine." She would proudly talk about her family while I wrote her prescriptions out. She never complained. During my second year at Cincinnati, Mrs. Folkner developed some serious metabolic disturbances (mostly involving her thyroid), causing her to become somewhat delirious. I admitted her to my team, but the hierarchy demanded that her primary care be assigned to one of my interns. I sought out my most capable and responsible intern and explained to him just how much she meant to me. Interns loathe new admissions because of all the work involved, but Miles was a very pleasant guy and he accepted this addition to his workload graciously. "You'll love her," I assured him.

It came to pass that Mrs. Folkner's problems got worse before they got better. She did well enough during the daytime, responding, "Just fine, doctor, just fine," when our ward team would round on her each morning—then she would go off to sleep for the day. Nighttime was a different story! Somewhere around midnight, Mrs. Folkner would fire up and become wildly animated, chanting "Sweet Lordy Jesus!" nonstop and at the top of her voice. Virtually all patients on her wing found it impossible to sleep and her incantation effectively rallied other demented patients, otherwise resting quietly, into action. The ward soon became a war zone.

The nursing staff had little choice but to move Mrs. Folkner to the otherwise vacant treatment room adjacent to the nursing station. Of course, the resulting commotion caused major disruptions to the function of the nursing staff—and their animosity, in turn, was leveled at the ward team responsible for the patient. Even more hostility came at us from ward teams covering our patients on the nights we were not on call. We were truly embarrassed!

Miles and I struggled with the dilemma for hours at a time. We felt that her basic problem was under proper treatment, but we weren't sure how long it would take her to respond. We were wary of using too much tranquilizer, for fear of doing her harm. Each time we would come into her presence during her incantations, she would look up sweetly and repeat "Just fine, doctor, just fine" as we left the room. After prolonged discussions with our attending physician, we cautiously initiated minor tranquilizer therapy at night. This, if anything, only served to make Mrs. Folkner even wilder. We finally resorted to Haldol, a major tranquilizer.

Standard doses of Haldol resulted in such a deep and prolonged period of sleep that even the nursing staff was concerned about over-sedation. Smaller doses produced only brief periods of rest and silence for Mrs. Folkner. As a last resort, Miles and I concocted what is referred to in medicine as a "sliding scale" dosage for Haldol. Commonly used to prescribe insulin for diabetes, the order is written to tailor the dose of medication given to a certain parameter in the patient (the level of blood sugar in a diabetic). It turns out that our only useful parameter for guiding the dose of Haldol for Mrs. Folkner was the frequency of her "Sweet Lordy Jesus" chants. Thus, the much discussed "SLJ sliding scale order":

for 3 consecutive SLJs, five Haldol 0.5mg IM STAT

for 4 to 8 consecutive SLJs, give Haldol 1.0mg IM STAT

for 9 to 15 consecutive SLJs, give Haldol 1.5mg IM STAT

for greater than 16 consecutive SLJs, give Haldol 2.0mg IM STAT

Mrs. Folkner did eventually go on to recover and later died of a stroke.

Rotations through the emergency department consisted of twelve hours on and twelve off. This not only seemed luxurious compared to the grueling rotations on the medical wards, but it also allowed for brief jaunts to Bloomington. It was always a treat to see my family and test the pizza and beer at some of my old college haunts. Later on, I was able to acquire tickets to Indiana University home basketball games and negotiate a few nights off to attend those sacred events.

With time, I found myself growing closer to many of my training mates than I could have imagined. The grueling weeks and months of mutual work and pressure hardened the bonds between us. I came to realize the truth in another of Paul Troup's axioms—"Ninety percent of what you learn in training will be from your fellow training mates."

When time allowed, Friday afternoons would find us packed into a University of Cincinnati hangout called Dollar Bill's. The tradition was irreverently labeled "liver rounds" and the nurses were faithful in their participation. These sessions went a long way in easing tensions and strengthening the delicate relationship between house staff and nursing staff, but invariably resulted in flocks of health care professionals babbling and staggering their way back to the hospital parking lot. I'm sure that the security guards were impressed by the sight of these educated drunks trying to find their way to their cars. Getting lost in Cincinnati was not uncommon for many of us—finding my way home on certain Friday nights was not to be taken for granted.

Post-graduate training, like college and medical school, flew by all too fast. Extending my training at Cincinnati to include a two-year clinical fellowship in pulmonary and critical care medicine, I found myself feeling empty when July of 1979 inevitably rolled around. It was time to leave for a new life in a new city.

Vivid memories follow me from Cincinnati; the night a fatal gunshot brought a Cincinnati policeman (along with half of the force) to the ER while I was on duty—and my emotions at watching the chest trauma resident literally rip open his chest and massage his heart with his gloved hands. It would be equally hard to forget the completely vacant ER waiting area (always packed) during the 1975 and 1976 home World Series games. But my fondest and most indelible memories are of you—the wonderful and ultimately competent people with whom I trained. Godspeed to all of you.

DR. RONALD ROBERTS

DR. RONALD ROBERTS
BECOMES ONE OF FIRST CERTIFIED
CRITICAL CARE SPECIALISTS
IN THE UNITED STATES

There's a brand new medical
specialty in Southeastern Indiana.
And this specialty is one many
metropolitan areas don't yet have.

This new medical specialty is
called critical care medicine,
and BCH's Dr. Ronald Roberts is
one of the first physicians in the
country to receive board
certification from the American
College of Physicians in this new
specialty.

Dr. Roberts is co-director of the
Hospital's Intensive-Clay Coronary
Care Unit. Dr. Roberts also is
board certified in pulmonary
medicine and internal medicine as
well as critical care medicine.

Discussing the new specialty,
Dr. Roberts said, "An intensivist
is a specialist in critical care. Until now, most intensive care units in
hospitals have been managed by internists, pulmonary or cardiology specialists.

"Now, there is a new speciality which has been established by the American
College of Physicians. These intensivists have state-of-the-art-training in
intensive care units," Dr. Roberts said.

The first board examination for the new specialty was held last November.
Although critical care training programs have been in place for over five years
now, the first three examinations are open to pulmonologists, cardiologists,
and internists who currently manage intensive care units. Of the estimated
3500 physicians who took the initial exam, a large proportion were in academic
(teaching) positions or recent graduates of a critical care training program.
Sixty four percent of theose physicians taking the examination were awarded
board certification.

"This is significant for the communities served by the Hospital. In the entire
country there now are approximately 2,200 board certified critical care
specialists in the entire country. With the number of hospitals in the
country, that means that less than one-third of them have a certified critical
care specialist directing their intensive care unit and most of these new
specialists are in big cities," Dr. Roberts said.

Bartholomew County Hospital Feature Article on Dr. Roberts

AN OPEN LETTER TO
MY COLLEAGUES

During a recent visit from my friend, Tim, the conversation took on a philosophical tone. This was only natural, as Tim epitomizes a side of me, and most of my colleagues, which we nurture all too infrequently. We like to think that we have a lot of Tim in us, but we invariably allow the pressures and expectations of life and medical practice to push Tim asunder. You see, Tim is the only physician friend I have who can visit for four hours without allowing the conversation to be drawn into the vast arena of what troubles the practice of medicine in 1991. Nary a negative popped up during our soul-sharing discussions of life, family, love, and medicine. Tim stirred a few Bob Dylan songs and quotes into the stew and the pot boiled over with tales of amusing encounters and rewarding relationships with patients and their families.

Tim is about my age, graduating from high school in Kokomo during the early sixties. He became a "child of the sixties" in every way except the drug-abuse stereotype, and he has held on. He practices medicine in the rustic setting of Brown County, Indiana, dresses and looks like he will be attending Woodstock after office hours, and loves to spend time rambling on with his patients about non-medical matters. Word is that he makes more than occasional house calls. Most of his patients that I know seem to consider him part of the family. He serves in some type of trustee role which involved him in helping a mutual patient of ours (of borderline physical and mental competence) purchase a used automobile. Apparently the clutch was an early casualty of our patient's driving technique, and Tim quickly

21

inherited the responsibility for repair—"I wish I'd been smart enough to buy him an automatic!"

Tim likes old houses, especially farms. He makes a point to visit patients or friends with farms on days that they are working so that he can pitch in and feel, rather than observe, the farm life. When he is not working or enjoying nature, Tim loves to collect old music and old stoves. He claims some expertise in evaluating, collecting, and restoring these relics of heating technology.

What can we learn from Tim? Aside from saving money on haircuts and clothes, learning what Tim is about imparts some truths about our reasons for being doctors. I've always prided myself in being good to my patients while trying to deliver sound medical care. And while cognizant of the need to generate financial support for family, education of four children, leisure time activities, retirement, etc., I'd like to think that I've never been driven by economic considerations. We certainly have cared for our fair share of medically indigent patients (some we even knew about in advance!).

Tim is about more than being courteous to patients and accepting a few no-pays into your practice. After an evening with Tim, I came to realize that my patients have done more for me than I could ever do for them. I have been privileged to be a part of one the few vocations on earth where people come to you with a willingness to share significant portions of their inner selves, their deepest and most personal thoughts and feelings. Most of these people trust you, some even respect you. These gifts are most often conferred upon you in advance of any signs that you hold a solution to their problem. Even more amazing is that many bestow their hard-earned money upon you, again in advance of proven solutions. Countless are the hours that I have spent with colleagues chuckling over amusing incidents and statements relating to our patients. And many more hours have I sat alone enjoying memories of moving gestures and comments reflecting the gratitude of my patients (and their families).

My twelve years of medical practice consisted of critical care, consultation, and primary patient care—on a solo basis and, for years, without adequate coverage. I well understand the frustrations of night call (after dragging in after a grueling day and evening), running behind, dictating in your sleep, missing meals (routinely), and losing contact with your family and friends. Those unfortunate enough to work or live with me will confirm that I bitched incessantly, cursed at what I perceived as inappropriate calls and pages, and frequently expressed disdain for the day that I decided to go into medicine. I agonized through the horrors of peer review, quality assurance, malpractice actions, and unfair practices of third party payors (or non-payors!). I lamented the burden of having to run a business while trying to devote my time and energy to the delivery of medical care. I loathed committee meetings and I've been heard threatening to assassinate anyone working for or associated with HCFA.

Now it's time to close my practice. Soon it will be time to die. I have to pause for a moment to ponder the meaning of all of this. Unlike so many of the mysteries of life, the meaning here is not clandestine or obtuse. The meaning is that I would happily do it all again. Competition for places in medical school twenty-five years ago was awesome. Medical training was demanding, fraught with frustration. Financial rewards have been progressively more elusive. But lasting, meaningful rewards have been abundant. I've been fortunate enough to spend my working days with the very finest people on earth. My colleagues as a group are industrious, capable, caring people who have dedicated their lives to being there for fellow humans in need. To a man or woman, I've seen sacrifice of self undertaken as a routine matter of life. Most of those people not only care about their fellow man, they have dedicated their talents, time, and energy to translate this care into action. The majority of nurses and hospital workers that I have known demonstrate the same qualities of caring for people and implementing this care into tangible help for those needing it.

Finally, I come back to the glue that holds all this together. The bottom line for the existence of all of us working in the health care field—our patients. In your times of need, and often despair, you bring so much into the delicate equation defining the health care team/patient relationship. You bring yourselves, all of yourselves.

My son is progressing through a premed curriculum at Indiana University. I have to tell him that the practice of medicine as I have known it will be a thing of the past during his career. I assure him that his financial rewards will be far more modest than mine and that the "hassle-factor" will undoubtedly increase. But there will always be patients, colleagues, nurses, health care workers—rewards and meaning.

I close with an idea attributed to Larry Bird at the occasion of his coming to terms with the Boston Celtics for his rookie season. Don't tell anybody (especially my patients!) . . . but I would have probably done all of this for nothing.

RONALD D. ROBERTS, M.D.
(1945 – 1991)
Memorial Scholarship Fund

Occasionally an individual comes along who makes us sit up and take notice. Such an individual was the late Ronald D. Roberts, M.D. His personality was unique because of his sense of humor, quick wit, and a nickname for almost everyone he knew. But Doctor Roberts was always able to laugh at himself as he was teasing and interacting with those around him.

He labored at many different jobs to finance his undergraduate and graduate educations as he worked to fulfill his dream of becoming a doctor. These jobs included newsboy and high school teacher. He was also an athlete, music lover, disc jockey, comedian, philosopher, and an ardent I.U. basketball fan.

He was a skilled physician and medical scholar devoted to continuing education, and he had board certifications in Internal Medicine, Pulmonary Disease, and Intensive Care Medicine. He had the ability to treat patients with dignity and respect. His sense of humor and honesty were valued by his patients, so many of whom had debilitating and incapacitating illnesses. His death at age 46 was a tragedy for his family and friends and a real loss for the local medical community.

In memory of this family man and loyal friend, a memorial fund to honor and perpetuate his memory has been established. The fund is designed to provide scholarship money to deserving medical students. The fund has been created by his friends, family, and medical colleagues.

The Bartholomew County Hospital Foundation is proud to be a part of this effort to honor Ron Roberts. The Hospital Foundation will supervise the investment of money given to the memorial fund and is including the Ron Roberts fund as a part of its 1992 annual fund drive. All money given to this memorial fund is tax deductible and will be used only for the provision of medical student scholarships. The actual selection of scholarship recipients will be supervised by a group of eleven advisory committee members who will work with the Foundation, but who will remain an independent group.

If you are interested in contributing to this fund, please designate some or all of your gift to the Ronald D. Roberts, M.D. Memorial Scholarship Fund on the enclosed pledge/gift form. Checks should be made out to: **Bartholomew County Hospital Foundation.**

An Open Letter to My Congressman

I grew up respecting authority (to this day I cringe with shame when pulled over by a traffic officer—in spite of playing with many local cops on the FOP softball team) and following rules. It seems paradoxical that I have little respect for elected officials. In fact, my feelings in the area would be more accurately described as cautious disdain.

I have few problems accepting the president of our country as a man worthy of my trust and respect. From Eisenhower through Bush, I found myself willing to be a loyal subject, rarely questioning policy or integrity. This held true even for democrats and presidents bent upon raising my taxes or sending me to Vietnam.

My reverence stops at the top, however. It seems that vice presidents have perpetually been invisible and/or the butts of jokes during my lifetime. This phenomenon fortunately attenuates considerably as these same men are elected into the office of the presidency. As we descend the hierarchy, my opinion of the performance of elected officials plummets.

Be specific, you say. Fair enough, I'll at least go over my greatest areas of disappointment. But first let me point out that my gripes are really more directed at a system than the people serving within it.

Lumping Issues: Any issue that is up for consideration in a legislative body should be discussed and voted upon for its own merits (or lack thereof). It appalls me to see bills passed into law that include one or more unrelated issues which have been "coat-tailed" onto the original vehicle for the apparent purpose of passing them into law without having to examine their merits individually. This, to me, amounts to disguising unworthy or unacceptable issues for the ultimate purpose of deceiving voting legislators, and therefore their constituency, into passing them into law. The end result is a law which has not had to stand the test of individual debate and vote.

Special Interests and Lobbies: Wherever there are funds in a public treasury there also congregate the legions of hopeful awardees of these treasures and associated benefits. Unfortunately, this process seems to have gyrated out of control in our present system, making it difficult for a common citizen to either negotiate a consideration or defend his/her tax base. Simply put, the average citizen has lost touch with "the system" while lawmakers find themselves targets of undue pressures from powerful and selfish forces.

Truths Never Spoken: Nowhere in our society is truth more a victim of silence than in politics. Examples would only serve to get me in trouble—but that is the mentality that perpetuates this injustice—"It would be political suicide to say that!" Occasionally, I do hear some brave soul point out to the organized opposition that healthcare is not a right. Like food and housing, compassion and morality argue that healthcare be available for all who need it (and I can agree with reforms in the system designed to achieve this goal). Nevertheless, healthcare is not, to my knowledge, addressed as a basic human right in our constitution. The matter is further complicated by the reality that a substantial percentage of our healthcare budget can be directly linked to willful abuse of substances known to be health hazards.

I'm also waiting for some brave soul to point out to gay activists that young people still die from leukemia, lymphoma, and other malignancies and disorders. Unlike most AIDS victims, virtually all of these folks had no lifestyle choice with regard to their disease. I would be far more sympathetic to a movement asking for more resources directed from areas of government waste and the private sector toward medical research and care of all killer diseases, especially those victimizing young people.

Having espoused these examples from a long list of grievances with our political system, let me admit the obvious. My knowledge of politics is, at best, rudimentary, and I am the son of a devout conservative. I will now apologize for taking your time, but not for my ideas.

Back row: Ron, Keith. Front row: Hazel, Mike, Charles

AN OPEN LETTER TO MY FAMILY

What a crew! A bizarre collection of devout individualists who have known me best and longest—and still manage to love me. You are not large in number, just rich in character and memories.

Ron, age 2

I suppose that the term "unconditional love" is most traditionally associated with that of a mother. Mom, you've seen me at my worst and at my best; you've seen me cower, complain, tell fibs, fink out on my chores, fight with my brothers, try to help my brothers, work and study without sleep, make teams, make grades, and, eventually, become a parent and succeed in a career. I never for a moment detected a lack of faith or love. I remember late meals after basketball practice, often with the added challenge of tag-along hungry teammates—you always handled it. Your dedicated protection of my sporadic sleeping hours while working through college made such a difference. And your uncomplaining contribution to our fragile family economy by taking in washing, ironing, and babysitting were never lost on me. You were surrounded and overwhelmed by four boys (Dad included in this category) and a male german shepherd, all doing their own things—but you always held it together for us.

Your natural innocence was under constant assault. Somehow, the worldly realities that you had to assimilate in order to deal with us heathens never so much as dented the beauty of your purity and innocence. You continue to stand out in the position of spiritual strength and faith in our family; so comforting to me at these times. What we did accomplish, much to my delight, is to transform you from a high school student, content to skip pep sessions and ballgames (I suspect that you had to be coerced into attending my high school varsity basketball games), into a sports junkie. Not just IU games (never miss), but high school games, other college games, and straining to pick up Reds baseball games on a fading, crackling AM radio station (even west coast games) have become your routine. I can't help but believe that this all evolved as another manifestation of a mother's love for the boys growing up around her!

Dad, you will always be Chester to us—you can thank your mom for starting it, but you've nurtured your image effectively through the years. You'll go into the record book for your blatant disregard for fashion and conformity ("Charlie's school of fashion"), your disdain for moderation (we've seen you drink the grease after frying bacon, and your sardine sandwiches with a whole stick of butter), and your proudly displayed Disabled Veteran license plates awarded for a ten percent sinus disability discovered during WWII. You thrive upon agitating Mom and anyone else who will lend you an ear. You've never met a stranger and I've never once seen you embarrassed (even while your sons were cringing with humiliation on your behalf). You routinely holler across the street to a stranger for directions to somewhere you know how to get to, and you think nothing of writing a sixty-three cent check at the Dairy Queen. Nonetheless, you always worked hard and kept the family afloat—usually holding down a minimum of two jobs. And no, you're not lacking in intelligence. I have vivid recollection of taking the civil service exam late in my college career so that I could join you working at the post office over the holiday rush. I was fresh from making As in calculus and trigonometry courses and was feeling confident to say the least. When I went for the hiring interview, the postmaster told me that I had done quite well on the exam. In fact, only one other employee had ever scored higher than me: Charles Roberts—my dad! Could this be the same man who later signed and mailed out a batch of sympathy and get-well cards to our friends at Christmas? (Oh, I guess I wasn't paying attention!) No, that was Chester!

In spite of the hard work and the Chester mystique, you were always there for us. Fishing and hunting trips, gardening, gathering wood, raising sheep, little league, Babe Ruth league, Monopoly, Scrabble, whisker kisses at bedtime—all engraved in my bank of pleasant memories. Your undivided support through my up and down athletic career, and later, my college, military, and professional careers has never failed to comfort me. And my greatest joys of all, those all-too-brief trips home from the service, medical school, or Cincinnati to bask in the presence and love of you, Mom, and my brothers. The non-stop pool games, complete with unrelenting bullshit and world-class fart contests interrupted only by laughter-filled meals, turned a three-day weekend into three hours for me. You made it all happen, Dad.

You were born Keith, but you've eventually evolved into "Bufford." I had things going pretty well for three years until you came along and shook Mom and Dad to the core. You started off headstrong—and it's only getting worse from there. Even during the years that I could physically subdue you, probably brutally at times, I never once changed your mind (no "uncles" in our fights!). Nevertheless, we remained close and fiercely defended each other from the countless outside aggressions directed our way because of the frequent moves of our family, featuring new schools, neighborhoods, and bullies. You later became wild—quitting high school, drag racing, working adult jobs, seeing adult women, fighting adult men—but you always remained loyal to me. And when it became apparent that you and Dad could not be in the same room without spontaneous discharges of megavolt electrical hostility, I knew that it would fall to me to work with you.

Our discussions were straightforward, simple, and absurd, as always. I convinced you (more accurately, you convinced yourself) to return to high school, then go on to get a college degree for the sole purpose of being able to present this document to those who felt the need to heckle you while you were sleeping off a drunk in a ditch. Sounded good to me. Things also went smoother after you went with me to the fraternity house and decided that most of these guys were not nerds and "pencil heads." Before long, you were highly revered as our best Little 500 bicycle mechanic and a member of the travelling workout team to Florida. Your college mentality was secured from that point.

Now you have that college degree and a master's degree in biology. You choose to build and remodel homes and consume mass quantities of junk food. I have no problem with this. You remain opinionated but fair, human, and kindhearted. You would do anything for any of us, and you often have. I could not ask for a better brother.

Mike, you managed to evolve into "Pisser"—possibly in part related to your preference for trees and garage corners to commodes. You came along nine years later than me (I think they finally gave up and decided to keep one of their miscarriages), so I didn't get to fight with you as much. Sure, you managed to get in the way, but you were pretty good about running along once admonished. Before long, your bones grew and you became one of us—the dreaded Roberts brothers. We'd take all comers in basketball, pool, beer drinking, and bullshitting. Our trips to the Indy 500 were classic. As time evolved, I think that it was your love of our home and family that made all of us want to be there every chance we got.

You were just reaching your own when I was hauled off to the army, never to live at home again. Every time I had to throw my possessions together and move, paint an apartment, or fix up a house, there you were, until the job was done. We had similar incomes and budgets (virtually non-existent), but you never needed money for your time or travel expenses (always featuring multiple major breakdowns). Somehow, my most expensive and nicest birthday and Christmas presents were always from you. Without so much as an "eat shit," you've always been there for me—never complaining and never letting your oversized heart show through your flannel shirt. Now you carry the torch to my sons. Thanks, Pisser.

Mike, a.k.a. Pisser

Harold Binkley, a.k.a. Bink

I could never leave the subject of family without pausing a moment with "Bink." You were born Harold Binkley to my mother's sister and served as my only older brother. The countless hours of roaming your farm, fishing, caring for livestock, gardening, hunting, and building boats that wouldn't float and houses that leaked (all native, nail-bending wood) fill a large volume of my childhood memory bank. Our barn loft basketball games were epic as were our admonishments upon your parents' return from work for failing to address our chores for the day. All was worth it with a delicious country meal followed by table games (no TV in those days) and the cozy sound of rain falling onto the tin roof of the converted chicken house that was home.

My most vivid memories call up two boys with rifles shivering at the edge of a pre-dawn woods—one of us, at least, wondering about the wisdom of leaving those warm sheets back at the house. Suddenly, the first rays of sun would begin to dance through the softly swaying branches of the tallest trees and the critters would strike up their chorus of morning. Shortly, the wooded hillside would become a blaze of color and adrenaline spurred us young squirrel hunters into action. I doggedly tried to keep up as you deftly made your way across the treacherous forest floor, frequently victimized by one of your riveting glances when I'd snap a twig ("We won't see a squirrel for hours, now!"). Then there was faking that I actually saw the "obvious" squirrel that you were patiently pointing out to me. You were too nice to ask me why a branch always blew off ten feet away when I finally pulled the trigger.

Eventually, the temperature and humidity would turn the woods into a steamer—it was necessary to shed clothes, much to the delight of those man-eating mosquitoes. About that time, our bladders began complaining. We must have appeared sophisticated while trying to swat hungry mosquitoes away from our most vulnerable goofies while trying not to get baptized with wildly flowing streams of urine. As I recall it, the sweltering conditions drove you back to the house ahead of me one day, leaving me with my one and only moment of revenge for your superior hunting skills. It seems that in your boredom, you shot a buzzard out of the isolated roost in the pasture. After listening to your howls and screams for a spell (I thought the heat had gotten to you), I went to investigate. What a sight you were, huddled beneath that tiny sticker bush while the flock of angry vultures hovered over you in formation, taking turns dive-bombing and puking on you! I could have enjoyed the moment more had it not been for fear. You sent me running to the house for a 12-gauge shotgun which finally served to extricate you from your chamber of horrors.

Through it all, we become brothers. I still won't forgive you for running and hiding from me—but you'll always be my brother.

AN OPEN LETTER TO SUZANNE

What kind of letter does one write the person who makes up the other half of you? The one with whom you share your most intimate thoughts and emotions—your lowest points and your highest? It would have to be a love letter.

You came into my life when I was fifteen years old. You were a chunky little thirteen-year-old with mischievous ways and a heart-stopping smile. Things weren't easy at first, if nothing else, because of our ages. I had to date your older sister (not that she wasn't attractive in her own way) just to get a look at you—and to get you to look at me. Double dates were imposed upon us, as well they should have been, and we had to be in early. Our lack of maturity allowed for only an awkward relationship, fraught with silly arguments, petty jealousies, and temporary break-ups. But we grew to love each other as we remained inseparable throughout my entire high school career. This love has not only endured, but grown, to the present time—surviving seventeen years of separation.

There are no words to describe the feelings of an adolescent boy upon experiencing his first *real* kiss, the first sessions of petting or fondling. To this day, I can pause and remember the exact songs crackling over the AM radio of my car as we drove and parked together. I recall with lifelike clarity the drives from your house to mine after being trusted to share your love without violating your innocence—my heart skipping wildly out of control while my testicles literally throbbed. I seriously doubted that you had an inkling of your magic power over me. Time and maturity only strengthened the bond between us. The hours that we were allowed together invariably passed in a blur—and we spent our hours apart plotting our next time together.

Graduation came for me and it was time to move on to college. Though I would be attending college in the same town, the writing was on the wall for me—we would inevitably have to part ways. I would not be allowed to attend your class party, the prom, or several other events so important to your high school career. We managed to hang on until the time of your class party in the spring of your junior year. With very little discussion, I accepted my fate of going on without you in March of 1964.

It took me approximately a year to get my life back in order, to find some semblance of academic and social success at IU. As determined as I was to stay out of your way, I found myself incessantly going out of my way to drive near your house or to walk where I thought we might cross paths. I took a job on the graveyard shift at the hospital wrapping and sterilizing supplies and helping out in the emergency room. I'm afraid that I wasted a significant amount of my employer's money gazing aimlessly out the window at the roof of your nearby house. I fantasized that I was working to support us as you slept in your tiny downstairs bedroom. Occasionally I would weaken to the point of sending out small gestures. I could never understand why you didn't respond—I still can't. Nevertheless, I came to accept that the flame in your heart for me had burned out.

The emptiness of those years turned to despair upon hearing that you were to be married during the fall of my senior year at IU. My successes in academics, the fraternity, and as a Little 500 bike rider seemed hollow and pointless. To make matters worse, my early performance at IU appeared to have devastated my chances of getting accepted to medical school. I soon found myself drafted into the US Army—leaving my beloved hometown at five a.m. on a drabby, ratty school bus for the induction station in Indianapolis.

I fell in love again—in a different way. My wife stood by me through the uncertain days of military duty, the more pleasant days of medical school, and the harrowing days of post-graduate training. Three beautiful children were born to us. Both of us worked and we were able to buy a home in Toledo, and subsequently, in Cincinnati. The time arrived for us to move to a new community and start a medical practice. But something was wrong—we had grown apart through the latter years. The love I once felt seemed to be missing; there was very little communication between us. We weren't even friends. The stresses of the move to Columbus only made matters worse. Soon I found myself working late just to avoid coming home to probable confrontation. We began to talk about the possibility of divorce.

I can't say that I hadn't thought of you almost every day since that fateful March in 1964, mostly daydreams and night dreams of our warm, innocent relationship when life was free and simple. I can say that contact with you was virtually non-existent for the seventeen years of our separation. My emotions upon hearing that you were splitting with your husband and moving to Bloomington overwhelmed me. The haste with which I established contact with you has left a lot of people convinced that we had something going prior to the demise of our marriages. Aside from the sparks from the old flames, we can rest comfortably with the knowledge that no contact existed between us.

Our reunion erased much of the pain from the years apart. There was little doubt from the (re-) start that if we could handle the pain of the official dissolution of our previous marriages, we would spend the rest of our years together. So through the trials of relocating and mixing families, we have renewed the bond that traces its beginnings to the summer of 1961. Has it been a "happily ever after" marriage? No, it hasn't—but then, yes it has!

Two people who spend virtually every hour of every day together—working, playing, parenting, sleeping—come to expect a lot from each other. When human imperfections surface, they are not well-tolerated. Communication is so abundant that the chance for miscommunication is greater. So it has been with us—we've had our great expectations and our miscommunications. But nowhere in the equation will you find no communication, no expectations. We long to share our time together—we detest our hours apart. We've remained lovers and we've remained best friends.

Time appears to be short for me at this point. The discomforts inflicted by my illness are far overshadowed by the thought of leaving you behind. It is so easy for me to lapse into anger with God for the precious years we missed sharing life together. The anger quickly melts into gratitude, however, as I thank God for the wonderful miracle of finding you again. Sharing life and love with you has made my life full.

Now it can be said—with final certainty. You have been the reason for my life coming together and you have been the glue that has held it together. Sure, I love God, my family, my children, medicine, basketball, nature … My reason for living, however, is to share everything that is me with my partner in life—Suzanne, I love you.

An Open Letter to My Children

There is a feeling of immortality associated with the birth of your children—the torch is passed onto the next generation; a part of you will live on indefinitely. It is a truly magic moment for a father who, unlike the mother, is able to totally immerse himself in the joy of the moment without the distractions of bodily discomfort. So it was for me—these emotional experiences unsurpassed by any that I've felt since.

Euphoria all too soon gives way to the reality that you are actually responsible for this slobbering, miniature humanoid. Moments of silly play and mutual admiration become occasional rest stops along a highway of sacrifice, hard work, and frequently, frustration. With passage of time the "little chip off the old block" takes on a personality and will of its own, often quite foreign to its noble heritage. That couldn't be my kid who piled his trousers during a sit-down dinner with a potential practice partner or cut loose with a thunderous fart during the sacred vows at a friend's wedding! Little league baseball and basketball games could often prompt an intense desire to master the art of disguise. Report cards and school open houses could evoke emotions of disappointment, rage, and embarrassment.

Little kids evolve into teenagers and past problems seem trivial in comparison with the new challenges. Insecure people are watching their childhood bodies metamorphasize into adult bodies—and are struggling frantically to find an adult person to fill them with. Parents and teachers become the enemy and peers become the most important forces in their lives. The boundless joy which I experienced at your birth seems a bit far off now.

Just when all hope seems lost, a new magic emerges out of hopelessness. You become a friend—a best friend. Through hours of soul-sharing discussion we learn that we've always been friends, but we had a role to play and we couldn't let on. Now we can drop the facades and share our lives openly and honestly. This time the joy of fatherhood overtakes me more gradually, like the tide moving in, rather than the big surfing wave of joy experienced at your birth. There is a feeling here that this going to be a far more lasting joy.

Carrie, I could not be there for your birth, but I've since come to feel that I was there in spirit. I was certainly there for your "rebirth" into the confident, productive, loving, caring person that you've become. What a pleasure it is to watch you bring smiles and positive vibes to virtually every person fortunate enough to be in your presence. Even greater satisfaction comes from watching you successfully conquering the challenges of higher education, without losing that sense of who you are or your keen sense of caring for others. I best remember our late-night talks (when else could you talk to me?) with the sharing of ideas that led us to understand each other. You've been a joy to me. You've been a friend and a daughter.

Scott, my first born, I think we've been buddies the whole way. Fathers and sons don't waste a lot of words; love is demonstrated through actions. So it has been with us. I believe that the only time I told you that I love you is when I let you fall down the stairs as a toddler and I was afraid that you'd have brain damage (still not sure!). But you know that I do, and I know that you do. I'm sort of glad that you didn't have to witness your normally cool and collected Dad trying to change a flat tire on that cold December Toledo interstate while your Mom was having labor contractions at two-minute intervals in the front seat of my old blue Cutlass. We pulled it out, however, and you came to join us very shortly after arriving at Toledo hospital. Your mother worked evenings so that I could attend medical school during the day. I was your babysitter at night, though it was never clear who was babysitting whom. I may never forgive you for saving your grump for me every night, spitting out those awful green baby food peas, and planting that turd in my brother's bathtub during our vacation to Florida. Now I watch as you negotiate your second year of premed studies at IU—far more successfully than I did it. I can see that you are going to do well and I can't help but feel pride. But most of all I remember the fun we had together.

Todd, you came on a beautiful, early April day in Toledo. I can remember the feeling of walking alone through the new green grass and daffodils of our backyard knowing that I now had two sons. The very next day, April 3, 1974, a devastating tornado ripped through Toledo and much of Ohio. This served as notice—Todd Roberts is upon us! I soon started my internship so I did not babysit with you as I had with Scott. Maybe that's for the best; your mom says you were a pistol. Sure enough, you grew into a boy with a mind of his own. Full of mischief, unable to hang on to a penny, underachieving in school—you have provoked more worry and concern from your parents than we could have guessed. So why haven't we killed you? Because you're fun and good. I've never seen a kid with a quicker smile or a softer heart. I've always noticed how good you are with animals, but more incredible is how you get on with little people. Even after you were old enough to drive, every little kid—of any age—who visits our home will not stop asking for Todd. And when you finally drag in from work or school, tired or not, you and the little people disappear somewhere until it is time for them to go—and they always file out the door repeating stories of Todd. You'll soon graduate from high school and I fear that you might not get into, or stay in, college. Not that college is the only answer. I know that you are an excellent mechanic. Whatever, I only wish you happiness, and that you always keep that little boy in you forever. You've been fun.

Laurie, you came while I was getting ready for a softball game in Cincinnati. Another rush job to the hospital, this time something new in my family—a baby girl. I didn't know how to act or what to say. Could Ron Roberts raise a girl? Only time will answer that troubling question, but all indications are that, perhaps in spite of me, you are turning out to be a wonderful young lady. I didn't know what to do at first, but I could tell early on that there was a definite difference picking up my little girl after a fall or comforting her when her feelings had been hurt. I remember hurrying to get home from work on time to awaken you from your afternoon nap. I would play *Music Box Dancer* on my stereo and you would hang on to the end of your bed and dance and smile while time stood still for me. But time doesn't stand still, and now you are an eighth-grader, full of energy and life, full of smiles. People are always saying how pretty you are, and it's true (of course I'm prejudiced), but I take my pleasure from seeing how pretty you are on the inside. You bring light to people; you bring them smiles. I see you care for other people. You have become a young lady before your time, but you still manage to live the full life of a thirteen-year-old. During my illness, you have never failed to come and cheer me up with a hug and a smile, and a poster. My fears at becoming the father of a little girl quickly vanish in your presence. I can only thank God that I was allowed to be your Dad.

Dads aren't perfect, and I was far from it. I most regret the many times I thought myself too tired or busy to spend time with each of you. Many times I wish I had spoken more from wisdom than anger, from patience than haste.

My greatest regret as your father is the obvious—allowing a marriage to fail and leaving you innocent, loving children to shoulder the hurt and confusion. Dying is nowhere as hard as leaving you children behind as I tried to put my life back together. For all you went through you have never shown me anything but forgiveness, understanding, and love. I am so thankful to you.

I feel that I've failed in getting across to you just how much of a role God played in my life. So many times I was hopelessly lost in trying to succeed on my own and I would turn it all over to God in prayer. Each of those times I would end up succeeding against all odds. There is a God and He will help you. Perhaps I feared turning you off to God by forcing the issue—this certainly happens. My way of dealing with this very important issue, perhaps less than effectively, has been to lead by example. You all know that I pray, attend church, and set aside a portion of my income and time to give back to God.

My belief that one of the greatest sins is to waste a talent that God has given us has led me to push myself relentlessly to become the best at what I feel God chose me to do. This is what I would ask of you—find your star and go after it with all of your might.

This brings me to a vital concept—toughness. It looks like things are going to be tough for you for awhile; tough to the point of not being fair. I know what it's like to work on through hopelessness and tears when everything around seems dark and hostile. This is what sets a Roberts/Brooks aside from the rest; we don't and we won't ever give up. The pursuit of our goals far overshadows any shit that comes our way as we make our way along. And in the final analysis, I can pass on to you that the old saying is correct: "The real pleasure is to be found in the journey toward our goals, not so much in reaching the final destination."

My philosophy of working hard for your goals in no way means that you shouldn't find time to play. Work hard, play hard! The ultimate prize at the end of all this is that elusive condition we call happiness. I believe that happiness is most easily found by those working diligently to accomplish their goals, especially if those goals involve helping others. But I am not the boss of the world (that's not what I've been telling you, is it?) and my formula may not be right for you. So, my children, I simply pray that each of you finds peace and happiness in your own way. Don't be afraid to talk to God along the way.

Laurie, Todd, Scott, Carrie—I love you.

In Memory of
Ronald D. Roberts, M.D.
(1945-1991)

Gifted Physician
Loyal Friend
Devoted Father and Husband
Lover of Old Time Rock and Roll
Charitable Supporter of Hospice

Area Deaths

Died Monday

Dr. Ronald Roberts
Funeral Wednesday

Funeral for Dr. Ronald D. Roberts, 46, of West Yokewood Court, will be conducted by the Rev. Anthony Underwood at 10 a.m. Wednesday at Asbury United Methodist Church. There will be no calling hours. Burial will be at Valhalla Memory Gardens in Bloomington.

Barkes, Inlow and Weaver Funeral Home was in charge of arrangements.

Memorials may be made to Asbury United Methodist Church, where he was a member, or to Bartholomew County Area Hospice.

Dr. Roberts died at 2 a.m. Monday at his home.

Born April 20, 1945, in Bloomington, Dr. Roberts was the son of Charles Chester and Hazel Mae Finley Roberts of Bloomington. He married Suzanne Jacobs April 3, 1983, in Columbus. She survives.

Also surviving are children, Scott David, Todd Ryan and Laurie Beth Roberts, and a stepdaughter, Carrie Ann Brooks, all of Columbus, and brothers, Keith F. Roberts of Ellettsville and Michael L. Roberts of Bloomington.

Dr. Roberts was a physician in private practice of pulmonary and internal medicine at 1655 N. Gladstone Ave.

At Bartholomew County Hospital, he was past chief, department of medicine, 1983 and 1984; past chief of medical staff, 1987; medical director, respiratory care department; and co-medical director, critical care unit.

Dr. Roberts also wrote articles for medical publications.

He graduated in 1963 from Bloomington High School, in 1968 from Indiana University with a degree in zoology, in 1974 from the University of Toledo with a master's degree in biology and in 1974 from Medical College of Ohio with a doctorate degree.

His internship and residency were at Cincinnati General Hospital and his fellowship at University of Cincinnati Medical Center.

He was a member of American Thoracic Society, American College of Physicians, Indiana Thoracic Society, Indiana State Medical Association and Bartholomew County Medical Society. He was a fellow of American College of Chest Physicians.

Dr. Roberts was certified by the National Board of Medical Examiners and American Board of Internal Medicine. He held medical certificates from Ohio and Indiana.

He was a U.S. Army veteran. He received the Upjohn Achievement Award in 1974 from Medical College of Ohio.

An Open Letter to the Grim Reaper

I hear you in the hallway outside my room at night. You seem content to watch and wait for the present time. Why not? Have I any choice but to come when you call? You are no stranger to me. My work brings me into your ominous presence more frequently than I've been able to accept. You've made brief passes at me in the past, only to back off for a time. And yes, I've always known you were coming for me at an early age.

Like most travelers on the road of life, I've had occasion to breathe up a prayer of thanks after an apparent narrow escape from the jaws of death. I was a twenty-one-year-old buck on my first commercial airline flight (New York to London), some 500 miles over the North Atlantic, when the pilot abruptly interrupted the cabin silence with a message ... "Ladies and gentlemen, I'd rather be whipped than tell you this ..." My life to that point passed quickly before my eyes as the message continued on to the effect that our aircraft had lost an engine and that we would be ditching two tons of fuel into the Atlantic, then turning back to NYC. We made it back without further incident, but my priorities were repeatedly rearranged that summer while drifting across Europe on a non-existent budget. My summer adventure was punctuated to a greater-than-normal degree with daydreams of being home with my family and friends.

I suppose most of us can recall similar incidents where death, even if briefly, seemed close at hand. I now appreciate the very definite difference between these rather fleeting visions of the Grim Reaper and the ordeal of receiving a death sentence such as a diagnosis of incurable cancer. The fleeting visions of your life passing before you play out over weeks and months, while thoughts of death pervade your daily activities—often shattering moments of serenity or pleasure. An innocent TV commercial depicting an elderly couple enjoying their grandchildren serves as a harsh reminder that you'll never see yours. Even more disconcerting is the relentless deterioration of your body and its functions, serving as a constant reminder that death is rapidly approaching. To witness the decay of a once proud and durable body is a sickening sight—especially when the body is yours.

I've seen a number of good people travel this road—some more graciously than others. I've come to believe that those who do it best are those at peace with their loved ones, themselves, and their maker. Without resorting to sermonizing, let me state without reservation that I am sustained immeasurably during these difficult days by the love poured out to me by family and friends, the knowledge that I gave my best along the way, and the comforting reassurance that can only come from a personal relationship with our Lord. My cup is far from empty.